This Journal Belongs To....

Carole McKenzie

Lockdown from April
2021

DATE...Thursday 22 April 2021

TODAY I AM GRATEFUL FOR ....

Doug's painting our 3 teak garden
benches with Danish oil!

_____
_____
_____
_____
_____
_____
_____
_____

ONE AMAZING THING THAT HAPPENED TODAY ....

Funny

Carrol Toulman's fridge magnet "No
man was ever shot by his wife while
washing the dishes"

_____
_____
_____

DATE...............................

TODAY I AM GRATEFUL FOR ....

_____
_____
_____
_____
_____
_____
_____
_____
_____

ONE AMAZING THING THAT HAPPENED TODAY ....

_____
_____
_____
_____
_____
_____

WHAT DID I LEARN TODAY?

DATE.................................

TODAY I AM GRATEFUL FOR ....

_____

_____

_____

_____

_____

_____

_____

_____

_____

ONE AMAZING THING THAT HAPPENED TODAY ....

_____

_____

_____

_____

_____

_____

WHAT DID I LEARN TODAY?

DATE.................................

TODAY I AM GRATEFUL FOR ....

_____
_____
_____
_____
_____
_____
_____
_____
_____

ONE AMAZING THING THAT HAPPENED TODAY ....

_____
_____
_____
_____
_____
_____

WHAT DID I LEARN TODAY?

DATE................................

TODAY I AM GRATEFUL FOR ....

_____

_____

_____

_____

_____

_____

_____

_____

_____

ONE AMAZING THING THAT HAPPENED TODAY ....

_____

_____

_____

_____

_____

_____

WHAT DID I LEARN TODAY?

DATE...............................

TODAY I AM GRATEFUL FOR ....

_____
_____
_____
_____
_____
_____
_____
_____
_____

ONE AMAZING THING THAT HAPPENED TODAY ....

_____
_____
_____
_____
_____
_____

WHAT DID I LEARN TODAY?

DATE................................

TODAY I AM GRATEFUL FOR ....

_____

_____

_____

_____

_____

_____

_____

_____

ONE AMAZING THING THAT HAPPENED TODAY ....

_____

_____

_____

_____

_____

WHAT DID I LEARN TODAY?

DATE................................

TODAY I AM GRATEFUL FOR ....

_____
_____
_____
_____
_____
_____
_____
_____
_____

ONE AMAZING THING THAT HAPPENED TODAY ....

_____
_____
_____
_____
_____
_____

WHAT DID I LEARN TODAY?

DATE................................

TODAY I AM GRATEFUL FOR ....

_____
_____
_____
_____
_____
_____
_____
_____
_____

ONE AMAZING THING THAT HAPPENED TODAY ....

_____
_____
_____
_____
_____

WHAT DID I LEARN TODAY?

DATE................................

TODAY I AM GRATEFUL FOR ....

_____
_____
_____
_____
_____
_____
_____
_____
_____

ONE AMAZING THING THAT HAPPENED TODAY ....

_____
_____
_____
_____
_____
_____

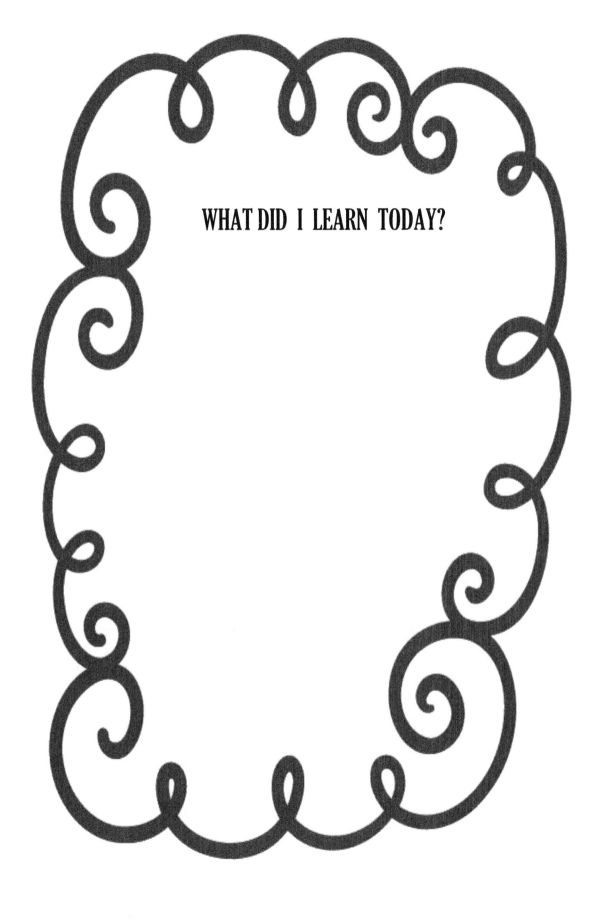

WHAT DID I LEARN TODAY?

DATE................................

My Happiness scale

TODAY I AM GRATEFUL FOR ....

_____
_____
_____
_____
_____
_____
_____
_____
_____

ONE AMAZING THING THAT HAPPENED TODAY ....

_____
_____
_____
_____
_____
_____

WHAT DID I LEARN TODAY?

DATE................................

TODAY I AM GRATEFUL FOR ....

_____
_____
_____
_____
_____
_____
_____
_____
_____

ONE AMAZING THING THAT HAPPENED TODAY ....

_____
_____
_____
_____
_____
_____

WHAT DID I LEARN TODAY?

DATE................................

TODAY I AM GRATEFUL FOR ....

_____
_____
_____
_____
_____
_____
_____
_____
_____

ONE AMAZING THING THAT HAPPENED TODAY ....

_____
_____
_____
_____
_____

WHAT DID I LEARN TODAY?

DATE.................................

TODAY I AM GRATEFUL FOR ....

_____
_____
_____
_____
_____
_____
_____
_____

ONE AMAZING THING THAT HAPPENED TODAY ....

_____
_____
_____
_____
_____
_____

WHAT DID I LEARN TODAY?

DATE................................

My Happiness scale

😃 🙂 😐 🙁 😣

TODAY I AM GRATEFUL FOR ....

_____
_____
_____
_____
_____
_____
_____
_____
_____

ONE AMAZING THING THAT HAPPENED TODAY ....

_____
_____
_____
_____
_____
_____

WHAT DID I LEARN TODAY?

DATE.................................

My Happiness scale

TODAY I AM GRATEFUL FOR ....

_____
_____
_____
_____
_____
_____
_____
_____
_____

ONE AMAZING THING THAT HAPPENED TODAY ....

_____
_____
_____
_____
_____
_____

WHAT DID I LEARN TODAY?

DATE................................

TODAY I AM GRATEFUL FOR ....

_____

_____

_____

_____

_____

_____

_____

_____

ONE AMAZING THING THAT HAPPENED TODAY ....

_____

_____

_____

_____

_____

_____

WHAT DID I LEARN TODAY?

DATE...............................

TODAY I AM GRATEFUL FOR ....

_____
_____
_____
_____
_____
_____
_____
_____
_____
_____

ONE AMAZING THING THAT HAPPENED TODAY ....

_____
_____
_____
_____
_____
_____

WHAT DID I LEARN TODAY?

DATE..............................

TODAY I AM GRATEFUL FOR ....

_____
_____
_____
_____
_____
_____
_____
_____
_____
_____

ONE AMAZING THING THAT HAPPENED TODAY ....

_____
_____
_____
_____
_____
_____

WHAT DID I LEARN TODAY?

DATE...............................

TODAY I AM GRATEFUL FOR ....

_____
_____
_____
_____
_____
_____
_____
_____
_____
_____

ONE AMAZING THING THAT HAPPENED TODAY ....

_____
_____
_____
_____
_____
_____

WHAT DID I LEARN TODAY?

DATE................................

TODAY I AM GRATEFUL FOR ....

_____
_____
_____
_____
_____
_____
_____
_____
_____

ONE AMAZING THING THAT HAPPENED TODAY ....

_____
_____
_____
_____
_____
_____

WHAT DID I LEARN TODAY?

DATE................................

TODAY I AM GRATEFUL FOR ....

_____
_____
_____
_____
_____
_____
_____
_____
_____

ONE AMAZING THING THAT HAPPENED TODAY ....

_____
_____
_____
_____
_____
_____

WHAT DID I LEARN TODAY?

DATE...............................

My Happiness scale

TODAY I AM GRATEFUL FOR ....

_____
_____
_____
_____
_____
_____
_____
_____
_____

ONE AMAZING THING THAT HAPPENED TODAY ....

_____
_____
_____
_____
_____
_____

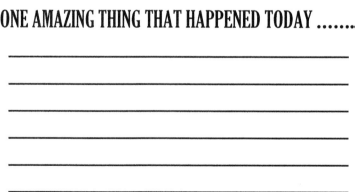

WHAT DID I LEARN TODAY?

DATE..................................

My Happiness scale

TODAY I AM GRATEFUL FOR ....

_____
_____
_____
_____
_____
_____
_____
_____
_____

ONE AMAZING THING THAT HAPPENED TODAY ....

_____
_____
_____
_____
_____
_____

WHAT DID I LEARN TODAY?

DATE...............................

My Happiness scale
😃 🙂 😐 🙁 ☹️

TODAY I AM GRATEFUL FOR ....

_____
_____
_____
_____
_____
_____
_____
_____
_____

ONE AMAZING THING THAT HAPPENED TODAY ....

_____
_____
_____
_____
_____
_____

WHAT DID I LEARN TODAY?

DATE................................

TODAY I AM GRATEFUL FOR ....

_____
_____
_____
_____
_____
_____
_____
_____
_____

ONE AMAZING THING THAT HAPPENED TODAY ....

_____
_____
_____
_____
_____
_____

WHAT DID I LEARN TODAY?

DATE...............................

TODAY I AM GRATEFUL FOR ....

_____
_____
_____
_____
_____
_____
_____
_____
_____
_____

ONE AMAZING THING THAT HAPPENED TODAY ....

_____
_____
_____
_____
_____
_____

WHAT DID I LEARN TODAY?

DATE...............................

My Happiness scale

TODAY I AM GRATEFUL FOR ....

_____
_____
_____
_____
_____
_____
_____
_____
_____

ONE AMAZING THING THAT HAPPENED TODAY ....

_____
_____
_____
_____
_____
_____

WHAT DID I LEARN TODAY?

DATE.................................

TODAY I AM GRATEFUL FOR ....

_____
_____
_____
_____
_____
_____
_____
_____
_____
_____

ONE AMAZING THING THAT HAPPENED TODAY ....

_____
_____
_____
_____
_____
_____

WHAT DID I LEARN TODAY?

DATE.................................

TODAY I AM GRATEFUL FOR ....

_____
_____
_____
_____
_____
_____
_____
_____
_____

ONE AMAZING THING THAT HAPPENED TODAY ....

_____
_____
_____
_____
_____
_____

WHAT DID I LEARN TODAY?

DATE.................................

TODAY I AM GRATEFUL FOR ....

_____
_____
_____
_____
_____
_____
_____
_____
_____
_____

ONE AMAZING THING THAT HAPPENED TODAY ....

_____
_____
_____
_____
_____
_____

WHAT DID I LEARN TODAY?

DATE................................

My Happiness scale

TODAY I AM GRATEFUL FOR ....

_____
_____
_____
_____
_____
_____
_____
_____
_____
_____

ONE AMAZING THING THAT HAPPENED TODAY ....

_____
_____
_____
_____
_____
_____

WHAT DID I LEARN TODAY?

DATE................................

My Happiness scale

TODAY I AM GRATEFUL FOR ....

_____
_____
_____
_____
_____
_____
_____
_____
_____
_____

ONE AMAZING THING THAT HAPPENED TODAY ....

_____
_____
_____
_____
_____
_____

WHAT DID I LEARN TODAY?

DATE..............................

My Happiness scale

TODAY I AM GRATEFUL FOR ....

_____
_____
_____
_____
_____
_____
_____
_____
_____

ONE AMAZING THING THAT HAPPENED TODAY ....

_____
_____
_____
_____
_____
_____

WHAT DID I LEARN TODAY?

DATE................................

My Happiness scale

😀 🙂 😐 🙁 😫

TODAY I AM GRATEFUL FOR ....

_____
_____
_____
_____
_____
_____
_____
_____
_____

ONE AMAZING THING THAT HAPPENED TODAY ....

_____
_____
_____
_____
_____
_____

WHAT DID I LEARN TODAY?

DATE................................

My Happiness scale

TODAY I AM GRATEFUL FOR ....

_____
_____
_____
_____
_____
_____
_____
_____
_____

ONE AMAZING THING THAT HAPPENED TODAY ....

_____
_____
_____
_____
_____
_____

WHAT DID I LEARN TODAY?

DATE.................................

TODAY I AM GRATEFUL FOR ....

_____
_____
_____
_____
_____
_____
_____
_____
_____

ONE AMAZING THING THAT HAPPENED TODAY ....

_____
_____
_____
_____
_____
_____

WHAT DID I LEARN TODAY?

DATE.................................

My Happiness scale

TODAY I AM GRATEFUL FOR ....

_____
_____
_____
_____
_____
_____
_____
_____
_____

ONE AMAZING THING THAT HAPPENED TODAY ....

_____
_____
_____
_____
_____
_____

WHAT DID I LEARN TODAY?

DATE.................................

TODAY I AM GRATEFUL FOR ....

_____
_____
_____
_____
_____
_____
_____
_____
_____

ONE AMAZING THING THAT HAPPENED TODAY ....

_____
_____
_____
_____
_____
_____

WHAT DID I LEARN TODAY?

DATE...............................

My Happiness scale

TODAY I AM GRATEFUL FOR ....

_____
_____
_____
_____
_____
_____
_____
_____
_____

ONE AMAZING THING THAT HAPPENED TODAY ....

_____
_____
_____
_____
_____
_____

WHAT DID I LEARN TODAY?

DATE................................

TODAY I AM GRATEFUL FOR ....

_____
_____
_____
_____
_____
_____
_____
_____
_____
_____

ONE AMAZING THING THAT HAPPENED TODAY ....

_____
_____
_____
_____
_____
_____

WHAT DID I LEARN TODAY?

DATE...............................

TODAY I AM GRATEFUL FOR ....

_____
_____
_____
_____
_____
_____
_____
_____
_____

ONE AMAZING THING THAT HAPPENED TODAY ....

_____
_____
_____
_____
_____
_____

WHAT DID I LEARN TODAY?

DATE................................

My Happiness scale

😃 🙂 😐 🙁 ☹️

TODAY I AM GRATEFUL FOR ....

_____
_____
_____
_____
_____
_____
_____
_____
_____

ONE AMAZING THING THAT HAPPENED TODAY ....

_____
_____
_____
_____
_____
_____

WHAT DID I LEARN TODAY?

DATE................................

TODAY I AM GRATEFUL FOR ....

_____
_____
_____
_____
_____
_____
_____
_____
_____

ONE AMAZING THING THAT HAPPENED TODAY ....

_____
_____
_____
_____
_____
_____

WHAT DID I LEARN TODAY?

DATE................................

TODAY I AM GRATEFUL FOR ....

_____
_____
_____
_____
_____
_____
_____
_____
_____

ONE AMAZING THING THAT HAPPENED TODAY ....

_____
_____
_____
_____
_____
_____

WHAT DID I LEARN TODAY?

DATE..............................

TODAY I AM GRATEFUL FOR ....

_____
_____
_____
_____
_____
_____
_____
_____
_____
_____

ONE AMAZING THING THAT HAPPENED TODAY ....

_____
_____
_____
_____
_____
_____

WHAT DID I LEARN TODAY?

DATE.................................

TODAY I AM GRATEFUL FOR ....

_____
_____
_____
_____
_____
_____
_____
_____
_____
_____

ONE AMAZING THING THAT HAPPENED TODAY ....

_____
_____
_____
_____
_____
_____

DATE...............................

My Happiness scale

TODAY I AM GRATEFUL FOR ....

_____
_____
_____
_____
_____
_____
_____
_____
_____
_____

ONE AMAZING THING THAT HAPPENED TODAY ....

_____
_____
_____
_____
_____
_____

WHAT DID I LEARN TODAY?

DATE.................................

TODAY I AM GRATEFUL FOR ....

_____
_____
_____
_____
_____
_____
_____
_____
_____

ONE AMAZING THING THAT HAPPENED TODAY ....

_____
_____
_____
_____
_____
_____

WHAT DID I LEARN TODAY?

DATE.................................

 TODAY I AM GRATEFUL FOR ....

_____
_____
_____
_____
_____
_____
_____
_____
_____
_____

ONE AMAZING THING THAT HAPPENED TODAY ....

_____
_____
_____
_____
_____
_____

WHAT DID I LEARN TODAY?

DATE...............................

TODAY I AM GRATEFUL FOR ....

_____
_____
_____
_____
_____
_____
_____
_____
_____

ONE AMAZING THING THAT HAPPENED TODAY ....

_____
_____
_____
_____
_____
_____

WHAT DID I LEARN TODAY?

DATE...............................

TODAY I AM GRATEFUL FOR ....

_____
_____
_____
_____
_____
_____
_____
_____
_____
_____

ONE AMAZING THING THAT HAPPENED TODAY ....

_____
_____
_____
_____
_____
_____

WHAT DID I LEARN TODAY?

DATE................................

TODAY I AM GRATEFUL FOR ....

_____
_____
_____
_____
_____
_____
_____
_____
_____
_____

ONE AMAZING THING THAT HAPPENED TODAY ....

_____
_____
_____
_____
_____
_____

WHAT DID I LEARN TODAY?

DATE.............................

My Happiness scale

TODAY I AM GRATEFUL FOR ....

_____
_____
_____
_____
_____
_____
_____
_____
_____

ONE AMAZING THING THAT HAPPENED TODAY ....

_____
_____
_____
_____
_____
_____

WHAT DID I LEARN TODAY?

DATE................................

My Happiness scale

TODAY I AM GRATEFUL FOR ....

_____
_____
_____
_____
_____
_____
_____
_____
_____
_____

ONE AMAZING THING THAT HAPPENED TODAY ....

_____
_____
_____
_____
_____
_____

WHAT DID I LEARN TODAY?

....

....

....

....

....

....

Printed in Great Britain
by Amazon